Crossed Paths

Snapshots of Life and Death by an
Undercover Hospital Chaplain

MAY CHEN, PhD

iUniverse, Inc.
New York   Bloomington

Crossed Paths
Snapshots of Life and Death by an Undercover Hospital Chaplain

Copyright © 2010 May Chen, PhD

iUniverse books may be ordered through booksellers or by contacting:

iUniverse
1663 Liberty Drive
Bloomington, IN 47403
www.iuniverse.com
1-800-Authors (1-800-288-4677)

ISBN: 978-1-4502-6454-9 (pbk)
ISBN: 978-1-4502-6455-6 (ebk)

Printed in the United States of America

iUniverse rev. date: 10/23/2010

Contents

Introduction:
How It All Began

Strictly speaking, I was never a "real" chaplain—at least not by profession. I first learned about hospital chaplains when I was a graduate student in psychology and participated in a research project that studied cardiac patients undergoing open-heart surgery. The study examined possible factors that contributed to postsurgical recovery, quality of life, and mortality.

As a research assistant responsible for patient assessment, I asked for an opportunity to observe an open-heart surgery in the operating room (OR). I wanted to get an idea of what patients had to go through in the process. Finally, the day came when I got to "play" and pretend to look like a doctor. They even gave me scrubs to put on! I didn't stand behind a glass window on a balcony as is sometimes shown on TV. I was there, five feet from the patient, sitting on a stool the staff so kindly provided for me. What unfolded before my eyes was certainly not as neat and clean as I had imagined it would to be.

The patient was barely conscious when they placed her on the operating table. There was no counting backward slowly until she lost consciousness. Nor was the patient covered up to her neck by sterile sheets. In fact, not an inch of her body could be covered while she was flipped and flopped from side to side and dark brown antiseptic was poured and painted all over her body. It was cold in the OR. I should have felt the cold for her if she were real. But I didn't. She didn't look real to me. When they finished prepping her, she lay completely naked on the stainless steel table, looking as if she were glazed in brown sugar syrup. The only indication of life was the sound of her heart beeping through the machine. This was before the operation.

The rest of the procedure was routine for everyone except me. I couldn't quite get accustomed to the burning smell when they cauterized vessels to stop the bleeding from the incisions. It was almost like the smell of a barbecue, but the feelings normally associated with that smell were rather different in the setting of an OR. The surgeons and nurses performed flawlessly as they prepared for the task of fixing the blockages in the coronary arteries that were preventing blood flow to the heart. They cut open the patient's chest, sawed through her rib cage with an electric saw, and poured a bucket of ice right into her chest. A bucket of ice!

They made a mistake! I thought to myself.

The surgeon glanced over and saw the look of horror on my face. "Hey, you!" he said. "What happens to a piece of steak you get from the market if you don't put it in the refrigerator? That's right, it rots! With blood to and from the heart being bypassed through the heart and lung machine, the heart is just that—a piece of meat without blood flowing through it." The ice kept the heart cool while the surgeon operated on it so it didn't decompose. Next, they made a long and deep incision on the patient's inner thigh to obtain sections of blood vessels. These would be connected and placed in the heart, creating a new route of blood flow to bypass the blocked coronary arteries and restore a healthy blood supply to the heart.

Although the surgery continued without incident, the

process was harsher than I thought. Needless to say, pretending to look like a doctor that day did not turn out to be as much fun as I had expected.

Anticipating an open-heart surgery can be scary and anxiety provoking. Recovering from such a major operation is also no easy task. Individuals may react differently as they progress through the process. Of the patients I assessed, some were depressed, some were terrified, and others were ready to face the challenge. But, regardless of how they responded to this life-threatening experience, many patients mentioned that visits from chaplains made a particularly strong impression and were helpful during their stay at the hospital.

What is a chaplain? I used to associate the term with an image of a man in uniform holding a Bible, delivering last rites to dying soldiers. After some research, I learned that at the hospital where I worked, chaplains were integral parts of the medical treatment team. In additional to regular visits to patients in various units, the chaplains were designated as members of the trauma team, taking twenty-four-hour on-call shifts, seven days a week. The chaplaincy program did not belong to any particular religion or denomination. Chaplains came from all religious backgrounds, including Protestants, Catholic, Jewish, and Eastern traditions. Perhaps the only common denominator among the chaplains was a belief in a higher power. They served people of all faiths and were there to help patients recognize and draw upon their own spiritual resources in times of need. My curiosity grew as I learned about these hospital chaplains. What was it about them that they were able to play such a significant role in the lives of people whom they had never met?

The Pastoral Care office at the hospital was a member of the Association for Clinical Pastoral Education. They provided training for seminary students in hospital chaplaincy. The minimum term of training was one year. I struggled with the decision to apply. Even though I was brought up in a Christian home and went to church regularly, I was far from being the minister type. In the end, victory belonged to curiosity. I applied with the recommendation of my church and was accepted into the program. They made an exception for me, the only layperson in the program.

And so it began—my one-year tenure as a "double outsider." As a chaplain, I was an outsider to the medical team. As a graduate student in psychology, I was an outsider to the chaplain team. I did not think or behave like other members of the medical or chaplain group, at least not in the beginning. However, being a double outsider provided me with a special window, a different insight into the lives of people whose paths I was fortunate to come across.

Part I:
ON THE FLOOR

Chapter 1
Representative of a Higher Power

My first day on the job was stressful. The chaplains in the program were assigned to different units throughout the hospital. In our assigned units we were to go from door to door, visiting every available patient on the floor. I was terrified of the prospect of walking into the unknown every time I knocked on a door. Basic information, such as gender, age, and reason for admission, was available to us from the computer and the charts. But it wouldn't tell the chaplains what kind of raw human emotion was waiting behind the closed doors. Nor would it give us tips on how patients and family members might react to a chaplain.

I wore a black suit and my official picture ID from the hospital that read "Chaplain May Chen, Pastoral Care," both of which were supposed to make me look and feel official. It took a while to find the unit I was assigned to. The hospital was a very confusing place to me, but I finally found the building and the floor. The elevator doors opened to a long, stretched-out hallway.

Instead of going from room to room in order, I looked at the bed census I had in my hand and wondered if it was possible to find an "easy" one for my first visit. I started screening from the top. I finally found a twenty-eight-year-old African American female who just had an operation to remove a cyst. She looked like a young patient with a relatively minor operation. Ms. Kimberly Glennon it was. I knocked on the door.

"Come on in!" she shouted rather cheerfully.

Definitely a good pick, I thought to myself.

"Hello, Ms. Glennon. I am Chaplain May. How are you feeling today?" It took me some time to associate "chaplain" with my name and a while longer to feel comfortable saying them together in one sentence.

She had a big smile on her face, "Oh, I am doing all right, Chaplain May."

"That's good! You look well; recovering quickly from the operation?"

"Yeah, still a little sore, but I started walking today. Never thought walking could be such a challenge!" She was animated. I nodded my head a little. But before I had a chance to proceed, she continued.

"You know, it's so good to see you, Chaplain. Sometimes I feel I can't talk to anybody. The doctors and nurses are really nice, but I can't talk to them." She looked away and paused. The look on her face began to change.

"When I was little, my uncle molested me," she said slowly. The cheerfulness from a second ago was drained from her face and voice.

"You—" I tried to take back the smile still on my face from just a second ago and figure out what had just happened.

"When I was nine," she continued, "I was raped by my cousins, because my father had molested their sister."

"Your—" still trying to process what was happening. I had heard from somewhere that repeating what someone said could be a good technique to use. But I was not able to get another word out before she spoke again.

"A few years later, I learned that I had contracted HIV from the rape."

"HIV—"

"I never confronted my father about it. But I think God is just. My father suffered a stroke that left him paralyzed and confined to a wheel chair for years. But, somehow he still managed to killed himself in the end."

"He—" I started to feel a little dizzy.

"Finally, I met this really nice guy a year ago who was very loving and supportive of me. He died of a sudden heart attack a few months ago. We were planning on getting married, you know." Tears were streaming down her face. Her pretty and seemingly jolly face from moments ago was now covered with tears, sadness, frustration, and anger.

For me, it seemed as if everything had turned into slow motion. I was completely disoriented. I had trouble finding words, and I didn't know what to do with myself. I didn't even know what hit me.

"Kimberly—" I called her by her first name.

"Call me *Kim*. It is so nice to see you, Chaplain. You see, God still cares about me. He sent an angel to take care of me. God, I feel so much better now … to let out all these emotions, and … to cry. I haven't cried in … I don't know how long! I always have to put up a happy face for others, because I know they don't really care about what is going on in my life."

She continued talking for a few minutes. I honestly can't remember what else she said. I was busy trying to pull myself together without showing it. In the end, I offered to say a word of prayer with her, during which she held my hands tightly. She cried, and then she laughed. She uttered "Thank you, God" before we ended the prayer.

"Thank you, Chaplain, you don't know how much this means to me; it's a miracle." A smile had returned to her face.

"You are welcome, Kim, and God bless you." As I walked out of the room, I thought to myself, *What did I do?*

Of course, the answer was—nothing! Yet, this woman allowed herself to be completely exposed and vulnerable in front of me in ways that she probably never would with anyone else. I would love to think that it was something about me: My black suit? My calming and inviting demeanor? But the question remains. Was it me? Or was it what a chaplain represented—God? The answer seemed clear. Some say people are God's instruments, through which others are loved, served, and cared for. That day, I did not feel that God worked through me. Still, he worked—in spite of me.

I had been completely fooled by Kim's cheerful greeting and big smile—as were the doctors and nurses. I stopped by the nursing station on my way out and left a note for the doctor to assess Kim for depression. As disoriented as I was throughout our interaction, some of Kim's behaviors and things she said led me to suspect that she might meet some of the criteria for that condition. I later learned that she indeed was suffering from clinical depression.

If I would have run into Kim in the elevator, at a checkout counter, or on the bus, I would have taken her smile and cheerful manner at face value. How many of the people we come across each day are hiding behind smiling faces, professional handshakes, or "I am fine, how are you?" statements? Now, I will think twice before resenting someone with a bad attitude. I will not be so quick to react to a rude or angry person. The truth is, you never know. These people may not be just annoying or simply having a bad day. They may be crushed inside or having a tough life. None of us would want to be that last straw.

Chapter 2
Listen

Doctors and nurses often put in special requests for chaplains to visit those patients who they feel may benefit from our visits. On this day, I had picked up a list of these referrals before my scheduled rounds. Mrs. Johnson—whose son, Michael Johnson, was here for a kidney transplant. I looked into the dark room before knocking. The patient was in bed with his back to the door. The blanket was pulled all the way up, covering half of his face. A woman was sitting next to the bed, dozing off.

"Mrs. Johnson?" I whispered. She opened her eyes immediately and looked up.

I introduced myself.

"Oh hello, Chaplain!"

"Is he sleeping?" I pointed to the patient, "I just wanted to come by and say hello—wouldn't want to disturb you."

"Oh no, he's awake. Come on in, please. Have a seat!"

"All right," I walked up next to the bed and saw that Michael had his eyes wide open, staring at the wall.

"Is this Michael?" He looked like a grown man to me. According to the chart, he was just over twenty years old.

"Yes," said Mrs. Johnson, combing her fingers through his hair—just about the only part of Michael's head that was not covered by the blanket.

"Michael, look, the chaplain came to see you."

Michael continued to stare at the wall, without a blink.

"What is Michael here for?" I pulled over a chair and sat down. Sometimes it was better to have them tell me why they were here.

"We are here for Michael's kidney transplant. We have been on the waiting-list for three years."

"I see. So this is what you have been waiting for." I noticed Michael was still gazing at the wall, without any expression or response whatsoever.

"Yes. But Michael is a little scared. It's okay, Michael, Mommy is here, and the chaplain is here to pray with us."

"Hello, Michael," I turned to him, "how are you feeling?" He pulled the blanket up even further.

"You know, he is autistic. He is all I have, and we take care of each other. Right, Michael?" He moved his body a little.

"He comes home every day; we cook together. He always makes sure that I take my medicine. I know he loves me. I will never forget the day he actually said 'I love you' to me." Tears came down her face.

"Sounds like Michael is very thoughtful."

"Oh yes, he is! He is the nicest boy, even though sometimes he is misunderstood. It was not easy growing up in our neighborhood. Many kids are into drugs and things. One time the police were chasing after some kids, and they jumped over to our yard. Michael was sitting on the front porch. The kids ran away, but the police dragged Michael down from the porch. He was so scared and started screaming. The police hit him real hard and put him in jail."

"My goodness. What did you do?"

"I was scared, but I prayed to God. He gave me the courage to go to court and fight for him. I showed the judge all of Michael's medical records. His severe medical condition required him to go for dialysis regularly. How could he be on drugs? They ended up letting him go."

"That must have been quite an experience for you."

"Oh, yeah. But God is good. You know, Michael and I read the Bible and pray together every day, don't we, Michael?" Michael remained very still in the bed.

"We have been through so much together, and we will get through this one together, too." She kissed him on his head.

I held their hands as I prayed for them. At the end of the prayer, Mrs. Johnson let out a big sigh and smiled.

As I left the room, I sensed and believed that a loving God was indeed watching over this partnership between mother and son. I don't know why Michael was born autistic. I don't know why they only had each other to hold onto. I don't know why their life had to be so difficult. But I did see her unwavering faith in the midst of a stormy life. I saw that the medical system did not fail Michael in giving him the kidney transplant that he needed. I knew Mrs. Johnson had the kind of relationship with her son that many mothers desire but never have. I saw Mrs. Johnson and Michael drawing strength from each other to build a world of love around them.

I have learned not to say much, even when I am not speechless. Listening without evaluating or reacting is easier said than done. In today's society, we can hardly be heard without being given advice to, express our feelings without having to hear other people's opinions about those feelings, or even vent without sensing another person's discomfort in what we have to say. Sometimes less is more. When family members or friends complain about a bad day, a frustrating experience, or tell us of their pain, instead of simply listening and acknowledging their feelings and experience, we are tempted to voice our own thoughts and feelings about what they say.

"Oh, you shouldn't feel that way."

"Don't be angry, it is really not worth it."

"What is the big deal?"

Most of us have the tendency to inject an evaluative element into our response: what we think they should do, and how we think they should feel. Instead of making the other person feel better, as we often intend to do, our reaction may cause them to feel misunderstood—that they now need to defend and justify how they feel, on top of feeling bad already. Try to observe your immediate reactions to what people tell you. See if you can catch your reactions before acting on them. It is an art of caring. I wonder if this is why Freud's psychoanalytic approach to therapy was originally called "the talking cure"? He emphasized the importance of a therapist being a blank screen for the patient. Being a therapist or not, the analogy is appealing. A blank screen reflects, but does not evaluate, what is being projected onto it. Perhaps we all need some room just to be heard.

Chapter 3
Can You Hear Me?

I was walking down the hall, making routine visits, when I heard noises coming from one of the rooms. I stopped by the room and saw an older gentleman in bed. He was intubated—a tube had been put down his throat and into the trachea to help him breathe. These tubes come in various sizes. They could be as small as the average household straw sold in supermarkets, or they could be bigger, more like the type of straw found in a milkshake from a fast food place. For most people, forcing a tube, large or small, down the throat is extremely unpleasant and can trigger some automatic reflexes. Therefore, sedatives are normally used for patients who have been intubated, to avoid gagging and to prevent them from pulling the tube out.

When I walked into the room, I saw the patient moving restlessly in bed. He was trying to make a sound, which was hard to do with a tube down the throat. A nurse also showed up in response to the commotion. Mr. Wilson, as he was listed on the bed census, grew increasingly agitated when he saw us. He was clearly gagging on the tube as he tried to sit up. The next thing I knew, the nurse was calling out for help, and several people appeared. Their immediate response was to hold him back and tie his hands down to prevent him from pulling the tube out himself, which could be very dangerous and harmful. Mr. Wilson reacted almost violently to the nurses' attempt to control the situation. His eyes widened with extreme fear, his hands waved up and down in the air, and his mouth moved as if he were screaming. But there was no sound except his heavy breathing, frequent gagging, and the bed sheet shuffling against the plastic cover of the mattress. His face was messy from crying so hard and drooling.

It was at this point that I walked up to Mr. Wilson, Mr. Howard Wilson.

"Howard!" I almost had to scream out his name to get the attention that I needed, and even that had little effect. But I continued regardless.

"You are in the hospital now. You can't talk, and you are gagging because you have a tube down your throat. It's there to help you breathe." He turned to look at me.

"I know you want the tube out, but you can't pull it out yourself. The nurses here are trying to help you." I motioned the nurses to stop forcing him down.

"You have to try to calm down for me, because the more upset you get, and the harder you fight, the worse you will feel. The nurses are here to help you. They will take the tube out as soon as possible, but you have to try to calm down. Don't fight them." Still breathing somewhat heavily, and still gagging, Mr. Wilson stopped fighting. Shortly afterward, the doctor was able to extubate him – take the tube out. He didn't have to be sedated or tied down before the extubation.

Imagine how shocking it would be to wake up one day in a foreign place. You open your eyes and find that you are surrounded by white walls, and on the white ceiling there is a flickering florescent light. It is cold in the room; you have on a loose, paperlike gown. As you try to get up, not only do you find that you are connected to these machines through wires, but you can't stop gagging. You can't remember exactly what happened or what brought you here, so you try to call for help. But you can't make a sound, because something is stuck in your throat. The harder you try to talk, the worse your gagging reflex gets. Finally, someone shows up. You try to get help, to get this thing out of your throat, this thing you think is killing you. But instead of helping, the person tries to pin you down. Then even more people show up, and together they try to push you down and tie your hands to the bed. You, too, would have fought the nurses as if you were fighting for your life, wouldn't you? I would.

I am not sure exactly what caused Mr. Wilson to calm down in the end. But I suspect he started to listen when he believed that he was being heard. In his frantic state, he was trying to communicate an urgent message—he was in what he believed to be a life-threatening situation, and he needed help. But his message was not getting through. Why else would the nurses ignore his condition and treat him as if he were crazy? Having someone repeat back to him what he was trying so hard to say—"I have a tube in my throat, I can't talk, and I am gagging!"—somehow conveyed to him that he was heard. In retrospect, it worked out that I didn't claim to understand what he was feeling or going through. I honestly couldn't have, since I have never been intubated. In fact, no one can understand precisely what another person is feeling or going through, even if he or she had been in similar situations before. People are different. Luckily, most of the time we are not required to know exactly what another person is going through. All Mr. Wilson needed was to know that someone heard what he was saying, not necessarily for someone to understand what he was feeling. Acknowledging his words and repeating them back to him probably did the trick. Listening is not really complete without speakers receiving confirmation that they have been heard, that their message has been received. Try not answering when someone calls out your name. Chances are that person would keep calling until you answered. The best way to stop the calling is to convey that you heard it.

Today when I conduct couples therapy, I often find one party's reluctance to acknowledge what the other has said. This almost inevitably causes the speaker to repeat him or herself, sometimes to the point of being annoying. Acknowledging that a statement or point of view has been heard is not the same as agreeing with it. Therefore, be generous in granting confirmations, even when you disagree. A useful statement would be "I hear what you are saying is ... though I do not feel the same way." Listening, when practiced correctly, is truly an active form of communication.

Chapter 4
Is There a Best Time to Say Good-Bye?

The attending physician of an eighty-year-old woman requested that I attend a "family meeting." This is when the attending physician meets with the patient's family to try to reach an agreement or a decision on specific medical issues. Mrs. Casper had been on the respirator for over a week now; she could not breathe on her own. Mrs. Casper had an Advance Directive (AD), sometimes called a living will. This is a legal document, prepared and signed by patients, that allows them to give instructions about the medical care they want to receive in the event that they become unable to speak for themselves because of serious illness or incapacity. There are various forms of an AD, but most forms consist of End-of-Life, Artificial Nutrition and Hydration, and Comfort Care instructions. Under an End-of-Life decision, a person may choose either to prolong life as long as possible using existing medical care, or not to prolong life under specified conditions, such as being unconscious with little possibility of regaining consciousness or having an incurable and irreversible condition that would likely result in death in a relatively short time. Under Artificial Nutrition and Hydration, patients may choose to receive "food" and "drink" that are necessary for life through feeding tubes or not. Under Comfort Care, a person may choose whether to receive treatment to alleviate pain, even if the treatment will prolong dying or shorten life. It is a standard procedure for hospitals to ask for an AD when patients are admitted to the hospital. For obvious reasons, patients are encouraged to have this document prepared, regardless of their age. The chaplains were encouraged to prepare one during their orientation.

In her AD, Mrs. Casper had clearly stated that she would not want to be kept alive on a respirator. Also in the AD were the names of two people she designated to make decisions for her when she could no longer express her will. Mary Ann, her youngest daughter was the first proxy, and in her absence, Jason, the second son, was to take her place. Mary Ann and Jason disagreed on whether to take Mrs. Casper off the respirator. Thus, the family meeting.

The room was packed when the attending physician, a nurse, and I walked in. The doctor briefed everyone on Mrs. Casper's condition: she remained unconscious and could not breathe on her own, and it was unlikely that her condition was going to change. Then the doctor read Mrs. Casper's advance directive, word for word: "These are my wishes if I am in a persistent vegetative state—I do not want life-sustaining treatment to be provided."

There was complete silence in the room. The doctor and I looked at each other and around the room. Everyone's head was bowed down; nobody looked up. The doctor wanted to say something, but I slightly shook my head. Give them some time. Taking Mrs. Casper off life support was to let her die.

These children were deciding whether to "let" their mother live or die. The hospital could probably get its legal department involved in trying to execute Mrs. Casper's AD, but efforts were always made to resolve problems within the family.

"I am ready to let her go," said Jason, without looking up.

Mary Ann burst into tears, covering her face with both hands. "Mom has always looked up to us when she was sick. She was recovering just fine a few weeks ago. She even sat up and tried to talk. I know some of you missed it, but I was there!" No one else spoke.

"Mary Ann, I see you don't want to disappoint your mother. What if she has a chance of getting better, right?" I tried to communicate to her that she was being heard.

"Exactly! But I am not God, and I don't want to play God! What should I do, Chaplain?"

Deserved or not, the role of clergy often comes with perceived authority. Members of the clergy can, and have been known to, take advantage of such perception. The doctor eagerly looked in my direction, hoping I would say something to nudge Mary Ann into making an "agreeable" decision. After all, she was the sore thumb that stuck out in the decision-making process. I looked Mary Ann in the eye—her pain was palpable. There was no "right" decision to be made. Whatever her choice was, she had to live with it. No logical reasoning or cost-benefit analysis could help her to make the decision or protect her from possible feelings of regret afterward.

"If your mom was sitting right here next to us, what do you think she would say?" I gently raised the question.

"Well, I know she wouldn't want to live on a respirator. But how do you know she won't wake up tomorrow?"

The doctor shook her head.

"Nobody knows. You are right; she might wake up tomorrow. But then she might not. Mary Ann, we are all here because we want to know what your mom would want in this situation. Unfortunately, we can't ask her now—nor can she tell us right now what she wants. She probably felt that you knew her the best, and that's why she designated you to speak on her behalf." Everyone else nodded.

"If she didn't know when she would wake up, she would probably rather go than live with a tube down her throat. But I don't want her to go!" Mary Ann could not stop crying.

Letting go is hard. Sometimes we hold on in the name of love, under the disguise of care. It takes great courage to do what we know is best for those we love even when it means watching them leave our lives. Most of the time, we have "the answer" inside of us—what we subjectively know to be the "right thing to do," even though there is no right or wrong in the objective world, where difficult decisions are often painted in shades of gray rather than in black and white. All we need is space. When we are given the space to process, to reflect, to be heard, and to come to terms with reality, "the answer" may surface without having to be searched for. You know you've got it when it comes with a sigh of relief.

A consensus was later reached by Mrs. Casper's family. Mrs. Casper loved to watch football. It was Super Bowl Sunday. Her family gathered in her room that night and watched the entire game with her before taking her off the ventilator. As we held hands and prayed together, the tension and struggle that were present in our earlier meeting could no longer be felt. Instead, the room was filled with a sense of peace that held and comforted each and every grieving heart.

Chapter 5
The Heart of a Prisoner

I was making my rounds, with the list of patients in my hand, when I saw two guards standing outside Mr. Jones's room. They didn't look like visitors, they looked "official." I looked up at these very tall and big men and introduced myself. (I don't know why police officers are always so big and tall, is that a requirement?)

"I am sorry, ma'am, but we cannot let you in." The officers were very polite. "We are under orders not to let anyone in, except for the docs and nurses."

"I see." I thought about it for a few seconds. "But I really would like to talk to Mr. Jones a little bit and just see how he's doing. May I do that from out here? Would you mind?"

"Uh ... I guess it's okay—if you don't go into the room." They moved aside to make room for me. I stepped up to stand right at the door. Mr. Jones was in bed but looking out to see what was happening.

"Mr. Jones—" I was about to introduce myself to him.

"Frank. And I know you are the chaplain; I heard you

talking." Mr. Jones, or Frank, was a very handsome young man in his late 20s. He was soft-spoken and appeared gentle in his demeanor. He was wearing a hospital gown and was clean-shaven.

A delightful young man, I thought to myself.

"Yes, Frank. How are you feeling today?"

"All right, I guess, given the circumstance." He shrugged.

"What brought you to the hospital?" I asked.

"Well, I have been having this pain, excruciating pain in my stomach. They couldn't find anything with the tests that they gave me. So now, they will do exploratory surgery to try to find out what's wrong. The surgery is tomorrow at seven in the morning." He waived his hands as he talked, causing the IV drip to flap on the stand.

"Explorative surgery to find out what's wrong?" That sounded scary to me.

"I don't know which one is worse. The pain is unbearable, but they are going to cut me open just to look around. I am also scared of what they will find. Cancer? Or something else that is going to kill me?" His anxiety and fear were surfacing quickly. His gestures became more exaggerated. I was afraid the IV stand would fall. I glanced over at the police officers from the corner of my eye; they didn't seem to be paying much attention to us.

"Frank, it does sound very scary—not knowing what is going on or what will happen. Your surgery is tomorrow morning. Would you like me to pray for you?"

Frank thought about it for a second, his eyes moved from looking in the direction of the door to staring at the floor.

"Yes," he whispered, almost as if he was talking to himself.

He looked back up at me, "Yes, but more importantly, can you pray for my wife and son?"

"Your wife and son?"

This was "more important"? I thought to myself, *after the fear he had just expressed?*

"Yes," Frank sat up straight, suddenly looking calm and determined. "My wife Jane and my son Eric—"

He took another moment before starting again, "He should be three now. I haven't seen them for a while, but I would like for you to pray for them—for God to watch over them and make sure they are okay."

After we prayed, Frank seemed relieved and at peace with himself. Something had happened to Frank when the word "prayer" or the image of God, or whatever the word might have meant for him, came into the picture. He was no longer concerned or afraid for himself. He was reminded of something "more important" as he put it, perhaps something bigger than himself. Religious or not, almost without exception I found God, or a sense of the divine, to be a powerful and sometimes transforming factor in the patients I saw.

Even the officers noticed. As I walked down the hall, they had switched guards, and one of them walked into the elevator with me.

"That was something you did. He seemed so different, so much better afterward!"

Something I did? I smiled and shook my head.

"What was he in for?" I asked.

The elevator opened, and the officer headed straight toward the coffee stand. Just before we parted, he answered, "First-degree murder."

Part II:
IN THE CALL ROOM

Chapter 6
Being On Call and Using Codes

"On-calls" are the worst. Usually a call shift is twenty-four hours—from 8:30 AM to 8:30 PM. During that time, the on-call chaplain is the one and only chaplain serving the entire hospital, from responding to staff referrals and emergency calls, to all "codes."

Learning the special terms and codes used in the hospital is an essential part of being a hospital chaplain. The on-call chaplain stays overnight at the hospital in a small call room, along with other on-call physicians. He or she carries the on-call chaplain pager, the number of which is posted on the big white board in the emergency department, as well as in all nursing stations. Just like the pagers of the on-call physicians, the chaplain's pager automatically goes off when there is a "code." A code is a hospital-wide command that activates a series of specific, closely monitored protocols.

"Code blue: code blue in the MICU, code blue in the MICU." When a patient is unresponsive, either not breathing or without a heartbeat or both, a code blue is called. When this phrase rings throughout the hospital intercom, the on-call physicians' and on-call chaplain's pagers go off within seconds of the announcement. A team of specialists drop what they are doing and race to the Medical Intensive Care Unit (MICU).

The code blue team is headed by a team leader. This person is assigned each day, for each shift, by the nurse manager in each unit. The team leader is trained and certified in advanced cardiac life support and is responsible for the patient's care during a code blue. The team leader is often a nurse from the unit. Another team member is the recorder, who monitors the patient throughout the procedure, documenting each procedure and the time the action is taken. The IV and meds person is responsible for establishing an IV and administering any number of medications designed to get the patient responsive. The airway team member establishes a clear airway to restore breathing. One team member performs cardiopulmonary resuscitation (CPR) if necessary. Often this person needs to trade off with an extra team member, as performing CPR can be exhausting. More staff members than those assigned to the code blue team answer the call and assist as they can. Overseeing the entire procedure is a physician. Also joining the team is a pharmacist and laboratory technologist when needed, and of course, the on-call chaplain.

Along with the trained personnel is the "crash cart." The crash cart is stocked with the medical supplies to revive a patient. Included in the cart are IVs, medicine, and a portable defibrillator, which delivers electric shocks to the heart and monitors the heart rhythm. The recorder is responsible for the crash cart. Crash carts are normally located in the emergency department, intensive care units, and in the operating rooms.

During the normal course of a day, team members work in

different departments throughout the hospital, but when called upon they come together, working as one unit to restore a patient's vital functions. A team of specialists is waiting for the call to save a life, twenty-four hours a day, 365 days a year.

"Code 40" activates a trauma team of trauma surgeons, radiologist, anesthesiologist, breathing specialist, radiology technician, lab technicians to draw blood, someone from the blood bank to bring blood, and of course, the on-call chaplain.

Usually, an ambulance or Life Flight helicopter notifies the emergency department (ED) by radio that they are bringing a patient to the hospital. The paramedics give a short history about the patient (age, problem, what happened), information about the patient's current condition (vital signs, such as blood pressure, pulse, respirations, temperature), and what has been done so far (CPR, oxygen, etc.). The hospital gives the paramedics further directions on what else to do to stabilize the patient (give them medications, start IV fluids) until they arrive at the hospital. Members of the trauma team all help to assess and treat the patient. This large group of doctors and technicians converge in the ED as soon as the code is announced, putting on gowns, gloves, and masks, and are ready when the ambulance or helicopter arrives. When it does, some of the ED doctors and nurses go out to meet it and help the paramedics rush the patient on the gurney into the shock/ trauma room located in the back of the ED. This room is separate from the triage that manages non-life-threatening cases in the ED.

"Code white" is an emergency code that applies to pediatric patients, which includes infants, children, and adolescents.

A code may be announced at any time throughout the

day or night. While different teams are designated to respond to different codes, the on-call chaplain is a member of all code teams. Contrary to regular rounds and floor visits, when responding to a code, the on-call chaplain mainly focuses on any family members who may be present at the time of the code. Watching a loved one being resuscitated, shocked, or poked with needles can be a devastating experience.

Chapter 7
"Have a Reasonable Night"

The signup sheet for on-call schedule was being passed around among the chaplains. I was thinking about my qualifying exam and therefore was not completely aware of what was going on in the room. The signup sheet had been around the room once already before getting to me. All of the dates were filled except one: Friday, February 13.

Hmmm … I'd rather not do a Friday, because it would require that I move a meeting around, I thought to myself.

"Can anyone take this day?" I asked.

No one answered.

"I will be happy to take another day," I said. Some looked up, others looked down at the floor, and a few exchanged strange looks with each other.

What was going on?

Suddenly, it dawned on me—but it couldn't be!

"Friday the thirteenth? Friday the thirteenth? Are you all kidding me? You are chaplains! Believe in God, not superstition!"

Some chuckled and moved around restlessly.

"I don't believe this! All right, I will take it!" I said, putting my name down in the slot. As a scientist in training, working in a scientifically and technologically oriented hospital, I absolutely refused to give into old wives tales and superstitions.

February 13, Friday. I arrived at the hospital at 8:25 AM sharp, taking over the pager from the previous on-call chaplain. As I went down to the basement level and walked into the on-call room, I saw a few doctors hanging out in the lounge area watching TV. The parting remark of the previous chaplain was still ringing in my ears, "Wish you the best, it will be full moon tonight."

As I learned from the doctors and nurses, one never wishes another a "good" call or "good" night, as that will surely guarantee a busy and sleepless night. "It never fails!" claimed a head nurse in the surgical intensive care unit.

A full moon? On Friday the thirteenth? What are the chances? I thought to myself as I used the chaplain's ID card to swipe open the little room with the "On-call Chaplain" sign on the door. It was a very small room with a bed, a desk, and a TV mounted up on the ceiling—almost like a college dorm, but smaller. I put down my overnight bag.

"Oh, come on, I am a chaplain, for crying out loud!" I talked myself out of feeling funny and shook off the little tingling sensation that was climbing up my spine.

As it turned out, we had thirteen traumas that night—a new record. The trauma surgeon closed off the trauma unit and even had to ask a medical flight transport that was on route to our hospital (a level I trauma center) to reroute to another trauma center instead. It was 4:00 AM when I finally had the chance to go back to the on-call room, take off my jacket, and slip into bed.

The pager went off. I struggled to get up and read the little screen.

"4:19 AM. Code 40. Ground. 4 min. Stab. CPR." It was 4:19 AM; a trauma was coming in by ambulance and was estimated to arrive in four minutes. The patient suffered from a stab wound, and CPR was being performed by the paramedics. I got up and got dressed quickly.

The patient had already arrived when I got to the ED. They opened up his chest right there in the shock/trauma room. A knife was stuck in his chest. Blood spilled everywhere. There were perhaps more than fifteen people in the room working on him. The trauma surgeon saw me and waved at me: "Come in, Chaplain! At this point, you are probably the only person who can save him!"

A few minutes later, the trauma surgeon walked out and took off his gloves. I understood that the patient had expired—another term used in the hospital to indicate that the patient has died. Expired, like a carton of milk. Whenever I heard this term, I envisioned all of us walking around with an expiration date on our forehead. The term may not be completely inaccurate after all.

Because this was a homicide, police didn't want the hospital to contact the patient's family. I went back to the call room, and fell asleep in my suit.

Thirty minutes later, I was paged to meet the family in the ED. As I walked out the door, another page came in that said, "We need you here, right now!"

The doctor had just delivered the news to the parents of the nineteen-year-old boy who died of a stab wound in the heart. "We tried to save him. We made an incision in his chest, but there was a big hole in his heart, and we just couldn't repair it."

The mother was crying out in disbelief. The father had a blank look on his face and not a drop of a tear. He was pacing back and forth in the non-urgent room; he did not want anyone near him.

I struggled to come up with something useful, helpful, or comforting to say, but nothing came to mind. I walked up to the mother, and she grabbed me, crying, "Oh God, oh Jesus, how am I going to take this? I am never going to see my boy again. I didn't know it was the last time I was going to see him when he left this morning."

After they had cleaned and covered the body (with the chest roughly sutured) and wiped up the blood in the room, I accompanied them to see the body of their son. The father slowly walked up to the body, took a long look at the son, and then gently pressed his cheek against the son's forehead. Tears were now streaming down his face.

The mother sat down by the son, touched his hand, and said, "Please open your eyes for Mommy, even it is for the last time." She started telling me "He's such a mommy's boy, so sweet. Whenever he comes home at night and his dad is out on night shift, he always comes to check on me."

"He had just gotten his hair cut yesterday," she added as she combed her fingers through his hair.

Then, inevitably, came all of the "what-if's."

"If I had only stopped him from going out with his friends this morning."

"If I had gone and picked him up when he called in the evening."

"Oh God, I would have picked him up from wherever he was …"

As a video playing back all the scenes through which a different outcome could have been derived, she tried so hard to will this into just a bad dream.

I was standing in the trauma room facing the entrance when the victim's sister hurried in. She thought her brother was hurt, but did not expect anything bad. She looked worried, but anxious to see her brother.

The mother looked up and said, "Your brother, he's gone."

The sister looked puzzled.

The mother was crying as she repeated "Your brother, he's gone!"

I wished I didn't have to see the transformation on the sister's face—from confusion, to lost, to searching, and finally, to realization. Minutes passed. She suddenly let out a long and loud scream, one that was likely to give anyone who heard it the chills—and then collapsed. She kept screaming, "My brother, they took my brother away! Oh God, this is not happening. This is the worst day of my life!"

I sat there with the family until another chaplain showed up for the next shift.

At 8:30 AM I finished my Friday the thirteenth, full-moon call. It was indeed a call from hell. Scientific or not—I would never again take another call on Friday the thirteenth. I squinted as I went through the revolving door to leave the hospital. It was so bright outside. The sun was shining, and I looked around after I adjusted to the light. It was a busy world. People were hurrying to get to wherever they needed to go. Kids were playing in the playground. It was a beautiful day. Life apparently goes on. I couldn't help but remember all the patients and families that came into the ED that night. Most had thought and expected that they would wake up this morning like everyone else, to carry on with their lives. What about that boy who was stabbed to death? For him, life was no more. For his family, life would never be the same.

Chapter 8
The Grand Finale

"Code blue, south building. Code blue, south building," the broadcast system announced throughout the hospital. It was completely dark in the call room, which was nice to facilitate sleeping anytime throughout the day or night. Most people liked to stay in the call room and get as much rest as possible, for you never knew when a code was going to be called. I could barely open my eyes when I turned on the light. The time indicator on my pager showed 2:30 AM.

Unlike most other staff members at the hospital, chaplains cannot show up in scrubs. Chaplains take care of people's spiritual needs, and people seem to associate clergy with certain ideals or images. Try to imagine your local church pastor sun bathing on a beach, riding on a motorcycle wearing a leather jacket, or taking a roller coaster ride. These scenarios just seem a bit odd, even though in our heads we know that clergy are people, too.

I got dressed and combed my hair so it wasn't all tangled and scary looking. Before walking out the door, I took a quick glance at the mirror to make sure I didn't look too sloppy. The south building was located next to the call room. It's a place of longer-term care relative to other units, such as the Medical Intensive Care Unit (MICU) or Surgical Intensive Care Unit (SICU). The patient for whom the code was called would have a flashing light outside of his or her room. Finding the actual room of the code was never a problem. A code team would have been on the scene already, and usually medical students and interns would come out of the woodwork to participate in the code. I recognized it as Mr. Troy's room as soon as I passed through the two heavy automatic doors, which were activated by the magnetic strip on my ID card. Mr. Troy was a man in his 50s. I had visited him on my routine visits, but he was never conscious. No one seemed to know anything about him. He had been in south building for over three weeks. I never saw anyone visiting him.

A crash cart was in place, with a cardiac monitor and defibrillator. The code team was doing everything possible to get Mr. Troy's heart to beat again. But he was "bleeding out," with no apparent cause. It was not a pretty sight. Blood seemed to be gushing out of every possible orifice in his body. The bed sheet was soon saturated with blood. I knew I could return to the call room since the patient was unconscious and there were no family members present. But something made me stay. For some reason, I felt that I was the only family he had. Finally, the team leader called the time of death. I walked up to the bed after most people had left. The room looked like a war zone, with towels, masks, tissues, and blood all over the place. A nurse stayed after to clean up the room.

So this was how he went. Alone. No friends or family. His "finale" was anything but grand. No one knew who he was, where he was from, or why he was there by himself. He might have been a father, a brother, colleague, or a husband. He might have been rich, or he might have been poor. He might have been a wonderful person, or he might have been a villain. Did he once love someone? Was he loved by anyone? In the end, this was where and how he left—in a room with strangers performing violent procedures on his body in an attempt to save him, in a room filled with the horrific odor of a mixture of medication, urine, blood, and other things.

Come to think of it, does it really matter where and how we die—or who is around? These may matter before death graces us with its presence. But when the moment finally arrives, each person is forced to face it alone, even those who are lucky enough to be surrounded by loved ones. It is a moment of the unknown and perhaps of fear. If it is unknown, what can we do to prepare for it? I can't help but wonder about the things that we strive for in our life—causes that we devote ourselves to, dreams and goals that we work hard to build and to achieve. Will they help us to prepare for that inevitable moment?

Chapter 9
What Can You Say?

I walked into the pastoral care office on a Thanksgiving afternoon. It was my turn to be on call. Today, it started at 4:30 PM. Instead of having a turkey dinner, I had one for lunch. After all, it was Thanksgiving. I was greeted by another chaplain who was eager to end the shift and begin the holiday.

"Anything I need to know about?" A routine question when changing shifts.

"Not really." She picked up her bag and started to walk out but then turned around as she remembered to tell me something, "Oh, just one. A fetal demise in room 308."

"A what?" I sometimes doubted my ability to understand English when I was in the hospital. The language and terminologies that were used in this already cold and foreign setting could be quite bloodless at times. "Fetal demise" is a term used to describe fetal death in utero, sometimes called stillborn. Fetal demise announces the death of a baby inside the mother's uterus.

It took me a while to locate the patient. Chaplains did not

make routine visits there, nor were they usually called into this unit. Some people know the maternity ward as the only place in a hospital blessed by the presence of joy and laughter. But bad things happen, even in there. Considerate staff members on the maternity ward had setup a system. For the patient who was losing a baby for any reason, a little card with a teardrop was posted on her door. This way, visitors and staff would be informed or reminded of the patient's condition before entering the room.

I knocked on the door before entering. The room was very dark, with the curtains completely drawn. The mother was lying on the bed. She had long, straight, brunette hair that was all wet and tangled from sweat and tears. Her eyes were swollen from crying. Her husband was sitting at the foot of the bed. He had on a pair of metal-framed glasses and a simple T-shirt and jeans. I later learned he was the clown of the family—the one who always made people laugh. When I greeted everyone, he tried to come up with a smile, but the look of extreme grief and his facial muscles attempting to pull up a smile made him appear almost eerie. Both sets of grandparents were present. You could hear a pin drop in this small and dark room of seven people.

Rebecca and Tom had been trying to have a baby for over two years. They were thrilled when Rebecca became pregnant. Hopes and expectations grew as they learned that the pregnancy was going well. Needless to say, a name had been picked, a room was setup and decorated, and toys were piling up for the various stages of the baby's development. The baby, Andy, was eight months and one week old today when an ultrasound indicated no cardiac activity. There was no sign or warning. The couple was simply here for a routine checkup. In fact, the day before they came for the scheduled checkup, the parents-to-be had called for an appointment with an accountant to discuss setting up a college fund. "We have to plan ahead you see, education is getting more expensive by the year," the proud father-to-be told his wife. Now, along with every other mother-to-be on the floor, Rebecca was going through labor. This was a drug-induced labor. She would go through labor like all the others—the contractions and pain. She would have to give every ounce of her strength to deliver the baby that she longed to meet. The difference was, however, that there would be no baby crying at the end of this delivery. There would be no shouts, tears, or any expression of joy after Andy was born. There would only be silence in Rebecca's household on this Thanksgiving evening.

Experienced chaplains caution to resist the urge to say something in situations like these. When tragedy strikes, it is surprising how often people succumb to the incredible pressure of unbearable silence.

"It could be worse."

"I know how it must feel."

"It's going to get better."

"You know, when I went through a difficult time—"

"It's God's will."

"I know of a person whose twin died."

And, my personal favorite: "This happened because God needed another angel in heaven."

The impulse to say something in these situations may be a reflection of our desire to be helpful, as well as our fear to be helpless. But, as we all know, the truth of the matter is that we *are* helpless, and that there is nothing we can say or do to improve the situation or to make those who suffer feel better.

Most of us cannot understand it, explain it, or change it. Feeding our own need to be helpful is not an objective in this situation. What we can do, however, is to acknowledge what has happened, and to tolerate our own feelings of helplessness, instead of acting upon them. What is far more important in this situation is presence: it helps more than words. Presence is being there completely *for* the other person, without having to address our own need to be helpful. Presence is what helps in sharing the burden or grief that is often too heavy for one person or one family to bear alone.

The grandparents from both sides had left, as they were physically and emotionally exhausted. I sat with the couple in the dark room until Rebecca went into delivery. It was after dark, but she didn't want the light on. They paged me to return upon Andy's birth and asked me to bless him. I held baby Andy in my arms on that Thanksgiving night, feeling all the weight of unrealized dreams, broken hearts, and lost love.

Weeks later, I received a letter from Rebecca. She was slowly recovering. In the letter, she said, "I don't remember what you said that night, but I remember you being there."

Being there. Some of the most important and meaningful messages may be best communicated through presence, not words.

Chapter 10
Dying Young

After going through the referrals that came in to request a chaplain's visit—some from patients or family members but most from nurses—I decided to visit a patient whose friend requested a chaplain. Looking at the patient's chart, I was able to get background information, which always helped. Alison, twenty years old, was hospitalized with metastasized cancer. Her religious background was simply listed as *Protestant*.

The elevator opened to the oncology floor. It was quiet, other than beeping sounds coming from various equipments. Some people were gathering around what appeared to be Alison's room. People made way for me as I approached. After introducing myself, I quickly scanned around the room. A rather large crowd. I was never good with meeting new people, and having to meet a lot of them all at once did not help with my anxiety.

It's not about me, I reminded myself, *or my own need to feel secure. It's about being there for the patient and family.* I took a deep breath, and this time slowly looked around the room, trying to make eye contact with everyone, nodding slightly as I acknowledged each person. Standing closest to Alison was an elegant, dark-haired woman in a blue dress, probably in her 40s. She looked tired, but peaceful. Standing next to her was a slightly older man in white dress shirt. He seemed agitated, almost angry.

"Chaplain, thank you for coming," the woman spoke. "Alison here, the doctor said she doesn't have much longer." When I looked into her eyes, a deep sense of sadness came through.

"Mrs. Tanaka?" She nodded. Then I looked over to the man next to her, "Mr. Tanaka." He shook my hand.

I bent down and touched Alison's head, "Hey, Alison, I am Chaplain May." Even with the help of an oxygen mask, she was breathing heavily. Very few strands of hair were left on her head. She slowly opened her eyes wider to look at me. Her eyes seemed so big now … relative to her sharp and thin face. She couldn't have weighed more than seventy pounds. Yet I saw signs of struggle in her eyes as she fought to take in each breath.

What does a chaplain represent to Alison and her loved ones? God? If they believed in God, they must have a million questions!

"Alison is a great girl," Mrs. Tanaka said. "She is an honors student, majoring in journalism. Captain of the swimming team. She is a wonderful girl." Tears began to stream down her face. Mr. Tanaka was visibly upset and left the room.

"We have a very large and tight family," another person spoke up, she was sitting at the foot of the bed. A beautiful young girl with shiny, dark, long hair. "We are twins, Al and I," she smiled "identical twins."

I was taken aback, almost as if I was the one gasping for air. Except this time, I took in more than just air. The smell of hospital disinfectants along with lack of air circulation made me nauseous. How could they be identical twins? I saw no similarities between the two. Of course, Alison did not always look the way she did on the last day of her life.

"Oh, she is such a fighter ... but ... she is in pain now ... so much pain," said Alison's sister.

"Chaplain, could you say a prayer for Al?" Mrs. Tanaka politely asked.

We all held hands together as we formed a circle. Mr. Tanaka came in to join us. Moments of silence followed as I ended the prayer, broken only by sounds of sobbing coming from various members of the family. I opened my eyes and saw very low numbers and almost a flat line on the monitor. A nurse came in to check on Alison's vitals and declared that she was no longer with us. Mrs. Tanaka turned to hold onto me and cried.

"She is in a better place now right?" she asked. "She is with God. She is no longer suffering or in any kind of pain, right?"

"Yes. Yes, you are right," I whispered as I held her tight.

They didn't doubt where Alison was going. They didn't ask me why: Why did a beautiful twenty-year-old girl with a promising future have to go so early? Why did she have to die this way? Why did this have to be such painful death for her—and her loved ones? Instead, they trusted. They trusted that Al was with God, and that it was a good thing.

Death is never easy, no matter where, when, how, or to whom it happens. It is especially hard, however, when it comes unexpectedly to unsuspecting or "undeserving" people.

It is an interesting psychological phenomenon. The notion of unexpected tragedies arousing special emotions in people was present as early as Aristotle's time. In Aristotle's *Poetics*, he emphasized our feelings of pity and fear in response to witnessing unexpected tragedies. The feelings of pity or sympathy and fear presumably correspond to the good in mankind and the bad in the human experience. Feelings of sympathy serve to unite those who suffer, and fear may serve to unite those unsure of what is to come. Aristotle even referred to these emotions as a species of pain. More recently, the psychology of "blaming the victim" also describes our desperate need to find a reason for life's tragedies and those it chooses to strike. We feel the victim must have done something to deserve the experience. In the end, if bad things could happen to good people (like ourselves), who is to prevent it from striking us?

Alison had hardly begun exploring life and all the possibilities that might be in store for her—which she never will know, at least not in this life time. An untold story, full of potential, yet unexpectedly cut short. I felt a unique species of pain in my heart.

Chapter 11
Are You Legally Married?

"10:17 PM. Code 40. Ground. 10 min. Stab in abdomen."

As I approached Trauma One, I heard moaning from an old man. He looked thin and pale, and there was quite a bit of blood on him. The trauma briefing board said, "Stab in the abdomen, self-inflicted." The pager went off again; it was the front desk of ED telling me that a family member of the code 40 was in the consultation room. It took me a while to find the room, as they had recently renovated the ED area. A nurse told me "good luck" as I walked into the room. It's usually in these rooms that family members receive bad news. When I entered the room, I saw an old woman sitting on the couch.

"Hello, I am Chaplain May, and you are Mrs. Frain?"

"Fraina, with an *a*. And we are not married."

"Oh, so what happened tonight?" I sat down next to her.

"Well, we were watching the game together. I got really bored, and so I went into my room to watch other programs. I usually don't let him leave my sight. All of a sudden, I realized it was quiet outside, no sound of the TV—he usually falls asleep without turning the TV off. I also heard him moaning a little. So I went out to check and saw blood on the sheets and blankets. Then I called the emergency people, and they got here within minutes. Is he okay, is it bad?"

"I saw him just now, and he seemed conscious. The doctors and nurses are doing their best to help him now. How are you doing? It must have been really scary for you." The woman looked rather calm and very much together.

"You know, this is not the first time he's tried it. Twice before. Cut his wrists and everything. He just got out of the hospital two days ago. He's been so depressed after he got sick. He used to be really active."

"Has he seen any psychiatrist or taken any antidepressant?"

"No, no psychiatrists, he wouldn't. But he's taking Paxel."

"He's got so many problems now," the lady continued, "including low platelets; he is taking medication for it."

"Did you tell the emergency people that?"

"I don't remember."

"Okay. Let me go and make sure the doctors know about it."

I went back to the trauma room, informing the doctors. Then I asked them if they could come out and brief the family member when they had a chance. They agreed.

I went back to the consultation room. This time, the old woman seemed to be in a zone—sitting alone, staring at the wall.

"They are still trying to help him and will keep you posted. So he was very active before?"

"Yes, used to swim three miles and run two miles a day. That's how we met you know, in swim meets."

"Really? How long are you together?"

"Over thirty-five years. We were both divorced."

"Wow, thirty-five years, huh? That's a long time. But you never wanted to get remarried?"

"Nah. I think we are still together *because* we never married. If we were married, we would just get divorced. He is seventy-seven, and I am eighty."

"No, really? And he was very active until he had an accident?"

"Yeah. He was swimming in the ocean and got hit by a wave. Fractured his vertebrae. I got a call from the hospital telling me that he was going to be paralyzed from the neck down. Even though he got better later, he can only walk with a walker. Then he had other problems. Recently he has been saying that he didn't want to live any more. The other day he told me to go ... it hurt my feelings. Even though I try to stay out of his sight, I want to be close by in case he needs me. I run my errands at four o'clock in the morning, so I can get back before he wakes up."

"You are very worried about him. Would you like to pray for him together?"

"Nah. I am too anxious and nervous."

"I understand," I said. "I think he is very lucky to have you. You must love him a lot."

"Thank you. At our age, it's not so much love, but caring. You know, I am divorced, and in the Catholic tradition I can't get remarried in the church or take communion again."

I paused for a moment and said, "You know, I think God wouldn't mind."

"I think so, too. I think God loves me."

"I do, too."

An hour had gone by, and no one came. I went back into the trauma room and was told that the patient had been sent to get a CT scan. When I asked for someone to come and brief the family member, I was told, "She is not his wife."

Stunned at this comment, I started walking back to the consultation room. On my way there, a nurse ran toward me and asked, "You know where a family member is?"

I said, "She has been here for over an hour, and I have been trying to get someone to see her." The nurse came with me, but I soon realized that she was there because she was in need of insurance information, not because she wanted to reach out to the family.

I went back and briefed Mr. Fraina's partner about the CT scan.

"So you used to be quite a swimmer, huh?"

"Yeah, I won metals and stuff."

Looking at her, it was hard to imagine what it must have been like for her when she was young.

"Really? What else did you do?"

"I was into dancing too and competed in championships."

"Wow, what kind of dancing?"

"Anything. Tango, waltz, you name it."

"You were a wild party girl!"

She laughed.

"I also used to dive into a lake. Different styles of diving. I must have been fourteen or something. Then I took over my mother's catering business, doing many other jobs at the same time."

I looked at her wrinkly face and glossy eyes. She was once fourteen, once young and wild.

"What is your name?"

"Molly, and his name is Winston, but I call him Wins."

"All right, Molly, he might be here for a while; you want to wait?"

"Yes, I will wait until the tests are over. I always stay by him and wait until they let me see him."

"Okay. Let me go and check what is going on."

I went back to the trauma room, asking them what I should do with Molly. They told me that the patient had already been sent into the OR for an operation.

"They don't need any signature?" I was shocked that Molly was not informed of this.

"Yeah, but she is not his wife. It went through administrative authorization. We need to contact his next of kin. She mentioned that he has two sisters?"

There is that phrase again—*she is not his wife.*

I went back to the consultation room.

"Molly, it seems that they decided he needs an operation. Do you remember his sister's phone number?"

"No, I can't remember. Forgot to bring it with me when I left. But they are not that close to us you know. I will call them and let them know as soon as it is not too early to call. I am the one who usually signs everything when he goes in and out of the hospital."

"Molly, do you have a power of attorney?" A power of attorney (POA) is an authorization to act on someone else's behalf in a legal matter.

"Oh, yes, I am so glad you mentioned that. I usually sign his name and put *POA* next to it."

"All right, so you would like to wait, right? Why don't you come with me to the surgical waiting room. It's a little bit more comfortable there."

I took her to the surgical waiting room; it was dark and she was the only one there. I turned on the TV for her and told her that it might take a few hours. I also showed her where the phone was and told her she could call the operator and ask to page the chaplain.

Then I walked out, called the OR desk, and asked them to please send someone to brief her after the operation.

"Well, she is not his wife," came the response.

I couldn't believe this.

"Okay, you keep saying that. They have been together for over thirty-five years, if anything, she is his common-law wife, and besides, she has a POA. She is now waiting in the surgical waiting room; please have someone come and brief her after surgery!"

"Well, the State of New Jersey does not acknowledge common-law spouses, but fine, we'll brief her."

The pager went off at 2:30 AM.

"The lady from the code 40 wanted to see you."

Maybe she just wanted to say good-bye. His situation didn't look very serious, and she was very together.

It won't hurt too much if I don't go, I thought to myself. I was so tired. But I tossed and turned and couldn't fall asleep anymore. Extremely tired, I mumbled as I got up and got dressed. With dry and red eyes, I found my way to the surgical waiting room.

Molly had tears in her eyes, "The doctor said he's not going to make it."

"Are you sure?"

"Yes. I saw him. He looked pale and all swollen. I kissed him, said good-bye, and told him that I loved him."

"Did they operate on him?" I was in disbelief, convinced the situation was not serious.

"Ah, I don't know, and forgot to ask. Do you think I can find out?"

"Of course!"

We went in. A nurse came and said, "You can't be here."

"She is the only family he's got, she has to be here!" I said.

The patient did have surgery, but they were unable to stop the bleeding. As a result of the stabbing, he had punctured his stomach, liver, and pancreas.

The pager went off again, "Code blue, surgical ICU." It had to be him, Mr. Fraina. I went back to Molly.

"Molly, something might have just happened—"

Before I was able to continue, she said, "I know, at this point, we are not talking days, but hours."

I went into surgical ICU and saw them performing CPR; his heart must have stopped.

I saw a flat line on the monitor as I heard, "Who is going to call it? Have you called it yet?"

Then waves appeared on the monitor again.

"Oh." It almost sounded disappointed. "Guess we are not going to call it."

I went out, informed Molly that Winston, or Wins was critical and asked if she wanted to see him again before she left.

She raised her head, straightened her back, looked straight ahead, and said, "No, I did that already."

Exhausted, Molly decided to go home and rest. As I walked

her out, she pulled out a ten-dollar bill with her trembling hand. "This is a little something for all your trouble."

My first tip as a chaplain. Of course, I declined it, and sent her off in a cab.

How was that eighty-year-old lady going to find the strength to clean up the blood-stained apartment? How would she find her way back to see Winston, if he survived through the night? What was her life going to be like without him? After all, "She was not his wife."

What does the institution of marriage mean? When God created Eve for Adam, did he hold a ceremony to "marry" them as a minister or justice of peace would do in most ceremonies today? Or did Adam and Eve sign a legal document as a contract of their holy matrimony? Molly and Winston did not have a ceremony. As for a legal document, Molly did have a power of attorney that afforded her most of the legal rights of a wife. However, in addition to religious and legal perspectives, there are also sociological and psychological facets to the concept of marriage. How does society perceive a married versus an unmarried couple? In Molly's case, she certainly was not treated as a wife, despite of the rights she was entitled to through the POA and the validity of her role as a wife to Winston. Though the sense of bereavement may be the same, the outside world may not extend the same generosity to significant others as it does to grieving spouses. And the amount of social support a person receives when losing a significant other may also be different. Is it any less legitimate to take time off from work to care for a significant other than it is for a husband or wife? Are the expected grieving periods different for a spouse than a significant other? Whatever our views on marriage might be, we must succumb to the fact that there is a distinction between married and unmarried couples on religious, legal, sociological, and psychological levels—a distinction that may come into play and result in important consequences at times when we are most vulnerable.

Part III:
NOT EXACTLY
A CHAPLAIN

Chapter 12
What Is a Chaplain?

I was about to take my first bite of chicken with broccoli, ordered from a nearby Chinese restaurant, when the pager went off. It read, "2374," an emergency department extension.

"Hello, this is Chaplain May."

"Oh, Chaplain, this is Anne from the ED, we really need you down here; a family member is freaking out, and we really need you down here *now*."

A family member being out of control in the ED—was this a job for the chaplain? Should I wear my chaplain hat? Or the psychologist one? Either way, I thought I should go and see what was going on.

I used my ID card to swipe open the doors to the shock/trauma unit. As the double doors swung wide, I saw a young girl in the hallway, standing outside of a treatment room, screaming. She was surrounded by several staff members.

On my way to the girl, I asked a staff member for an available private consultation room near the ED. After securing a room, I walked up to the girl.

"Hey!" I shouted.

The girl turned around and looked at me. That seemed to have gotten her attention—when everyone was hush-hushing, someone shouted louder than she did. She looked angry but otherwise fine, no tears or signs of devastation. She was probably around sixteen years old and looked a little thin; she had long dark hair and seemed about my height. I took a quick glance—she didn't have any shoes on, just white sports socks.

"I am Chaplain May. I know you want something. But you will have to stop shouting. Try to be calm, and then tell me what it is that you want, okay?"

"Fine! I just need to use the phone and call my relatives to tell them about my dad!"

"That sounds like a reasonable request, and we can do that. Why don't you come with me."

She seemed a little surprised, and still looking guarded, she slowly followed me to the consultation room. "I may have to make long distance calls, you know," she said, as if she was testing me, but no longer shouting—thank goodness!

"That's fine," I said. I got an operator on the line, identified myself, and requested an outside line. Then I handed the phone to her, "Here you go. Make your calls, and I will be right back, all right?"

She nodded, but still didn't trust me judging by the look in her eyes.

I went out to get some information on the patient, the girl's father. The doctors were administering electric shock to his heart as I walked into the room. The patient had a clean cut mustache; his face was literally blue. *That really doesn't look very good*, I thought.

"What's the story?" I asked a nurse.

"He came in by ambulance that responded to the 911 call. He came in with cardiac arrest, but we were able to get his heart beat back." A doctor chimed in, "The pattern of his EKG looks really bad, and we can't seem to get it out of that pattern."

I stood there for a moment and then walked back to the consultation room. I knocked before entering the room; the girl was just finishing a conversation. After she hung up the phone, I sat down across from her.

"Do you need anything? Water?"

She shook her head.

"What is your name?"

"Amy," she almost whispered. All those energy she had before, they were gone.

"Amy, what happened today?" I looked at her in the eye. She looked less guarded, but instead, a little lost now.

"We just came back from India a few weeks ago. Everything was fine … well … not exactly fine—my parents are fighting a lot; they are getting a divorce. My dad, he has been very stressed lately. I am just very scared." Her eyes began to well up. "Recently, whenever I do something wrong, he says, 'You will be very sorry if I die tomorrow.' And he has been having chest pains. Do you think he's going to be okay?"

"I don't know, Amy—" My pager went off again. It was the ED. "Amy, stay here, I will be right back."

I quickly walked over to the nursing station and was informed that Amy's father had just passed away. Amy was the only family present at the hospital, and the doctor needed to inform her. I asked to speak to Amy first, just to prepare her a little bit.

I went back to the room and sat down next to her this time.

"Amy, remember the doctors who were helping your dad when you came into the hospital?"

She nodded.

"They want to talk to you about your dad. Is that okay?"

Immediately, she looked alarmed. She sat up, straightened her back, and said, "Yeah."

The attending physician came in and gave her the news, "We tried very hard to save him … his condition was too severe … despite of our efforts—"

Amy was extremely well-composed throughout the briefing. Afterward, she said some family members were on their way to the hospital and requested to be left alone until they came. Before I left, I put my hand on her shoulder, and we looked at each other. I am never very good with kids or teenagers, but I think we connected.

I went back to the call room lounge, picking up my cold chicken with broccoli. I no longer had an appetite. Something about Amy's situation struck me. What kind of parent would tell his daughter, "You will be sorry if I die tomorrow"?

I was not sure how much time had passed before I was brought back to reality by yet another page. Some of the doctors in the lounge took an extra look at me. Chaplains get that sometimes. We are not like them, and no one is really certain how we fit in. We don't wear scrubs or white coats, yet we share call rooms with the on-call doctors.

I was called down to the ED. Apparently, some of Amy's relatives and family members had arrived. Amy was screaming again—and kicking this time. Everybody was shouting and crying, and more family members were on the way. The nurse told me that Amy had been shouting for "that lady in black suit" to come back. When I got down to the ED, all the consultation rooms were unavailable. With the help of a very kind nurse, I was able to take Amy into an unoccupied patient room outside of the ED.

The room was a little dark. It was an autumn evening. You could see the sun setting through the window; most of the leaves from the trees outside had fallen. It seemed a little chilly outside. Inside the room, Amy closed the door and plopped herself on the bed. She had tears all over her face.

"I don't want to be with those people [relatives]. They don't know anything, and they always want to tell me what to do. They don't know anything!"

"Amy—"

"My dad, he was supposed to take me to see colleges. We had all these appointments. What am I going to do? I should have called 911 sooner and not listened to him."

"What happened today, Amy?"

"My dad has been having chest pains for over a week now. But he kept on saying that it's okay. This morning, he called me from his room. I went in and saw him breathing heavily. He said his chest was hurting and asked me to rub his back for him. I did. But he didn't get better; the color of his face changed, and he began to throw up. He wanted me to get him a bucket. I was scared and said I wanted to call an ambulance. But he said, 'Not yet, I know, I will tell you when to call.' I was so scared. His faced turned dark, and he couldn't breathe. I started crying—that's when he pointed to the phone and told me to call 911. My brother and mother were still home when I came with the ambulance." She curled up on the bed, against the wall.

This whole thing sounded so very strange. But this was not the time, the place, or my role to look into the incident.

"Do you blame yourself for listening to your dad?"

"I don't know …"

"I think it is very hard *not* to listen to our parents in emergencies like this; they know better than we do."

"That's true. And my dad, he's a professor—he knows a lot. And he's the only one who cares about me going to college. That's why he set up appointments for me to meet with college counselors."

"Really? What kind of professor was he?"

"Toxicology."

Something clicked in my head, and things began to make a little sense.

"Can I please stay here and not go with them?"

"Amy, unfortunately, you are a minor, so you cannot really stay here without supervision from a family member. Besides, your family really needs you now."

Some of Amy's relatives came in looking for her as we spoke, urging her to leave with them. I had a knot in my stomach as I watched Amy get out of bed and be ushered out of the room with tears in her eyes and her white sports socks as her shoes.

She turned around as she walked out. "May? What is a chaplain?"

I looked at her and managed to squeeze a smile on my face. "A friend," I said.

Amy kept looking back as she walked down the long, busy, seemingly sterile emergency department hallway. I watched her disappear behind the double doors, wishing that there were something I could do.

A few days later, I heard that because of the somewhat mysterious and unexplainable nature of his death, the hospital requested an autopsy be performed on Amy's father. Amy's mother declined the request at first, but Amy somehow convinced her mother to agree, which I imagined to be no easy task given the family's cultural background, Amy's age, and her standing in the large family. Amy was an exceptionally intelligent and independent young woman. I don't know what happened afterward, but I believed that Amy was ready and able to face whatever her father's autopsy eventually revealed.

Chapter 13
A Detective

It was a somewhat quiet Sunday afternoon when a code 40 (trauma) was called. A male patient, probably in his 30s, came in with stab wounds. He was barely conscious; aside from some weak moaning and groaning, he couldn't respond to any questions. Soon after the patient arrived, a family member rushed in. She was short, around the same age as the patient, and had shoulder-length dark hair. She was panicking and looked lost, which was understandable. A hospital is a very intimidating place, especially in the back of the emergency department where the shock/trauma unit is. Doctors and nurses are usually in scrubs or surgical gowns, and many would have masks and gloves on if they were treating patients. People might hear screaming in one room, or soft moaning coming from patients "parked" on the side of the hallway, in wheelchairs, on a gurney, or in a mobile bed. The constant beeping sounds in various tones, pitches, and tempos could almost form a symphony of their own. Not to mention the background in white, and the hospital smell. I suppose it should be a clean smell, such as the combination of bleach and alcohol that all hospitals have. If you have ever been to a hospital, you know what I am talking about. The "clean" hospital smell, however, can be hard to bear sometimes. Ironically, most of the time people are exposed to such an environment when they are most vulnerable, physically, psychologically, emotionally, and perhaps, spiritually.

"Does anyone speak Spanish? Can we get someone who speaks Spanish here?" a staff member called out.

Spanish, I thought, *shouldn't have a problem finding someone*. In the meantime, while the trauma team was treating the patient, the family member stood outside of the room, in a corner, still looking lost and scared. Not speaking the language made the situation that much worse. I walked over, pulled up two chairs, gestured her to sit before I sat down next to her. She looked at me helplessly, wanting to say something.

A lot of questions were going through my mind. Who is the patient? What's his relationship to her? What happened? Who stabbed him? If it's a fight, should we be expecting more people?

The doctors' and nurses' voices were coming through from the treatment room.

"Hey, stay with me here!"

"What is your name, sir?"

"You are in a hospital now; we'll take care of you!"

"Do we have a name here? Anything? Driver's license, medication, allergy? Get me someone who speaks Spanish for goodness sake!"

I went into the treatment room briefly to get an update of the patient's condition. The stab wound was not serious, it seemed he was going to be all right. They just didn't have any information on the patient. Usually people would come in with personal belongings in their pockets, such as a wallet or a cell phone, something we could use to identify and learn more about them. Not this patient.

I walked back to the woman. She seemed eager to tell me something. I looked at her in the eye, raised my eyebrows, opened my eyes wide, and smiled—trying very hard to create a reassuring look.

"Looks like he is going to be okay, don't worry." I put my arm around her and tried to convey a sense of hope and comfort. She looked at me; I wasn't sure if my nonverbal communications were effective. But she was still trying to say something to me.

This time, I tried to gesture complex questions, such as "What is his name?" and "Is he your family?" by pointing to the room and drawing all sorts of arrows in the air. I have never played charades, and this was probably not a good time to start learning how.

"*Robo!*" Now she just looked irritated and frustrated. Where was the Spanish-speaking interpreter that we needed?

"What—is—his—name?" I pointed to the patient once more. This time I tried to really enunciate by speaking louder and slower, as if that would help me to be understood, which was just silly. It's as if you don't speak Greek, and someone tries to make you understand a Greek sentence by shouting the words to you slowly. The problem is that you don't understand the language, not that you are hard of hearing or stupid. So charades were not my thing, and Spanish was not my language; what else was there to do? Show-and-tell? That's an idea. I took out my own wallet, showed it to the woman, pointed to the patient, raised my eyebrows again, this time with a big question mark in my look—at least what I had hoped to be a question mark in my look.

The woman responded enthusiastically this time. She pointed to the patient and took my wallet from my hand. Gesturing to stuff the wallet in her pocket and acting as if she had a knife in her hand, she "stabbed" me and then turned around, swinging her arm upward in a semi-circle, demonstrating what I interpreted as "gone," "took off," or "ran away." Could this be a robbery? Now *that* was show-and-tell!

I caught up with the emergency medical technicians (EMTs) who had brought in the patient just as they were on their way out. I found out that they picked up the patient in a Laundromat just a few blocks away. Because the patient was a stabbing victim, the police were notified. I greeted the police officer who came, and I told him that this was a possible robbery case. Given the close proximity of the hospital to the crime scene, the suspect might not be far—especially if the suspect "ran away" instead of "drove away" as was indicated by the show-and-tell I had participated in earlier. The police officer acted quickly and called for more units to search for the robbery suspect.

When I was about to walk back to the woman, my pager went off again. I needed to attend to a dying patient and her family in Medical Intensive Care Unit. The Spanish-speaking woman and I looked at each other from across the hall as she was about to enter the treatment room to see the patient, and I was about to exit the Shock/Trauma unit. She had seen me talking to the police. She no longer seemed agitated; she even had a smile on her face when she waved good-bye—or was it "hello" or "thank you"? Regardless, she waved at me with a smile.

Later that day, I heard that the police had apprehended a suspect for a robbery and stabbing that occurred in the local Laundromat. I was quite amazed. So much could be achieved by simply making oneself available and being with a person in need, even when you don't speak each other's language. The outcome might not always be what you would expect, but it is almost always meaningful.

I was not a chaplain this time—heck, I was a detective!

Chapter 14
An Observer

It was two thirty in the morning. I was on my way back to the call room after responding to a code 40 when I saw an older woman sitting in the hallway. It was a cold winter night with temperature far below freezing. The ED was quiet after they stabilized and moved the code 40 patient upstairs to surgery. The woman had a full set of silver hair that glistened under the fluorescent light. She was at least in her mid 60s and had on a heavy gray sweater underneath her winter coat. She was just staring into the air.

"Hey there, are you okay?" I stopped by just to check.

"Huh?" She looked up at me as if brought back to the present by my question. I sat down next to her so she didn't' have to look up.

"I just want to see if everything is all right. What are you doing here?" Aside from her apparent state of confusion and the fact that she was in the emergency department at 2:30 AM, she looked okay to me physically.

"My friend," she pointed to a room, "got into a car accident. But the doctor said she was going to be fine."

"A car accident? You were out driving at this hour? Where to?" It must be an emergency of some sort.

"To Pennsylvania from New Jersey. There are four of us," she said.

"Four?" I looked around. There was hardly anyone there other than the nurses on duty and this lady's friend in one of the rooms.

"The two of us," she pointed to her friend and herself, "were going to Pennsylvania to pick up a dog—a dog we got from the rescue shelter there. It's her birthday you see, and she has always wanted a dog. We looked everywhere, everywhere, but we couldn't find a suitable one. Then two other friends of ours in Pennsylvania found one. We were going to drive down to pick up the dog, and the four of us were going to come back together. We drove two cars, just in case one car wouldn't fit the four of us and a dog. We couldn't wait, you see. We had to all get together and get back with the dog by her birthday."

I saw the spark and excitement in her eyes as she told me about what happened. It was a big deal to her and all her friends. It was important that this task be accomplished by a deadline—her friend's birthday. But in reality, what happened on this cold winter morning was that two old ladies, no, in fact, four old ladies, decided that they could not wait to take a road trip; they had left after midnight to pick up their friends and a dog so that they would make it back in time to celebrate one of their birthdays. They had to do it today, and they had to do it immediately. It was way below freezing outside, and water had turned into ice on the road.

Her wrinkled face was serious and childlike at the same

time. I knew she would argue with me if I were to lecture her or tell her the potential danger that could be involved in their collective decision. She had already made it crystal clear, "We couldn't wait, you see. We had to all get together and come back in time."

I brought her in to see her friend, who was lying in bed with a walnut-sized bump on her forehead. She pulled up a chair next to the bed and started talking. Between the two of them and a few pairs of reading glasses, they quickly managed to figure out how to dial from a cell phone. Of course, they did not call their husbands or children. They called the other two girlfriends who were eagerly awaiting their arrival in Pennsylvania.

There is something about friendships among women, something that can be unique and qualitatively different from any other relationships. I suspect that this was such a friendship. The friendships among these four ladies sustained and rejuvenated them as they entered old age. I saw no difference between these women and a group of middle school girls in the way that they supported and counted on each other, in the way that they faced the world together as a group. That early morning, in an unusually quiet ED, I saw four kids playing. They were laughing and crying with each other at the same time, completely unaware of what was going on around them. Even a big, shiny, bruised bump on the head could not ruin their party or discourage them from going after what they wanted. Seeing so much love and free spirit among these kids, I walked away quietly. I did not have the heart to break up their party.

Afterword

The human experience is a complex one. It is enriched by our interactions with others. It is heightened in our vulnerability. A hospital is one of those special places where many complex emotions emerge. Some people face unexpected life-changing events in a hospital, others confront impossible choices. For those who make it out of a hospital, the experience often makes them pause and perhaps reflect, if ever so briefly. It is a window through which the core of human emotions is intensified and magnified. As an outsider, I was privileged to be invited onto the center stage of each unique story—not as an actor, director, or audience, but as a presence.

Sometimes, we forget the importance of being. We are busy thinking, planning, engaging, and playing the various roles that life bestows upon us. Too busy thinking about what to say to a friend in pain, we are not there to share the grief. Too busy giving advice to someone in distress, we stop listening. Too busy doing things for our loved ones, that we forget we may be missed. *Doing* is important. But *being* is called for in extraordinary times. Walking alongside someone through a difficult journey may be more needed than trying to change the packaging of the experience—or adding ingredients to it.

Learning how to love and care for our fellow travelers in this lifetime is a challenging task. But it can be done. With a little bit of effort, good intentions, and a lot of practice, we can all become better listeners, caretakers, and lovers. We all need to learn to slow down, especially when we feel nervous, and take time, especially when we feel lost, not knowing what to do or say. Being with the negative emotion of helplessness may be harder, but it is more important than working to get rid of it. No emotion will last forever, even when we feel like it might. Staying with the experience, and letting it take its course (rather than trying to change it or run away from it), is an option worth considering.

Today, I remain cautious not to take a cheerful tone or smile at face value. Many people assume we are too busy to care or listen. My original momentary curiosity was transformed into the experience of a lifetime. As I continue my journey in pursuit of understanding human behavior, I will always remember the lesson that struck me during my very first visit as a hospital chaplain: I don't have the answers. Luckily, we don't have to know in order to care. We just need to be truthful to our thoughts and feelings, and most importantly, to be genuine in our presence with each encounter.